On the tı
of
WRITERS IN SUSSEX

Michael Lane

S.B. Publications

For my wife

First published in 1996 by S. B. Publications
c/o 19 Grove Road, Seaford, East Sussex BN25 1TP

ISBN 1 85770 092 9

Typeset by CGB, Lewes
Printed and bound by MFP Design & Print,
Longford Trading Estate, Thomas Street, Stretford, Manchester, M32 0JT.

CONTENTS

ACKNOWLEDGEMENTS

Extracts from the poems of Hilaire Belloc are reproduced by kind permission of Peters Fraser and Dunlop Group Ltd, the verse by T S Eliot by kind permission of Faber and Faber. The photographs of A A Milne, Virginia Woolf and Henry James are reproduced by kind permission of the National Portrait Gallery. Other photographs are by the author, who would particularly like to thank the owners of Crabbet Park for their permission to photograph the house.

ABOUT THE AUTHOR

Michael Lane is a one time scientist and teacher who has spent a considerable time exploring the highways and byways of Sussex in search of the great writers and the homes in which they lived. He lives in Surrey and has broadcast on literary anniversaries in that county and in Sussex on local radio.

INTRODUCTION

IF you are on holiday in Sussex - or indeed if you are lucky enough to live there - then this book is for your enjoyment. The county is rich in famous writers, and many of the houses they lived in are open to the public. The books they have written, the stories and characters they have created and their own colourful lives are full of interest and entertainment. In some of the surroundings their presence can almost still be felt. Looking for them throughout the county gives the searcher another excuse for enjoying, as they did, the beauties of its landscape and villages.

This book is set out as a series of trails which make interesting and scenically attractive journeys by road. Each route is a suggestion only, and its starting and finishing point a matter of choice. The intention is to link writers to their surroundings.

Parking places are indicated and times and admission charges, together with a telephone number for further information are given in respect of properties open to the public. In addition, the Ordnance Survey Landranger maps (about one and a quarter inches to the mile) are strongly recommended for the extra detail they pro-vide. However, you should just be able to manage with a good road atlas such as the Ordnance Survey three miles to the inch Motoring Atlas.

I have chosen writers who worked in this century, so they are suffi-ciently recent to be real presences. Their books are still on library shelves and on sale in editions of classics. Some have been given a new lease of life in television adaptations, and some are never out of print. I hope that after using this book you may feel inspired to dis-cover (or rediscover) the delights of the bookshelf. But I have not assumed in the book any detailed knowledge of the writer and so I have given a brief sketch of each author's main work.

Most have had strong bonds with Sussex and have written about it. For some, like Belloc and Kipling, it is a major influence in their lives, though only two, Wilfrid Blunt and Sheila Kaye-Smith, were

5

actually born here.

Many of those who are Sussex by adoption moved here at a time when authors felt they needed to be part of the London scene but wanted the peace and tranquillity of the countryside. The rural isolation they could find in Sussex was just a few steps away from the convenient railway stations. It was the equivalent of the present-day house in Provence – and had the same drawback that it might attract other city-based writers to spoil the view, something Virginia Woolf complained of at Rodmell.

In addition to the eight trails that I describe in detail I have included a section of briefer mentions of those whose links with Sussex are slighter or whose connections with the county are before the middle to end of the nineteenth century. Alfred, Lord Tennyson, for instance, divided his later years between Farringdon on the Isle of Wight and Aldworth House, high up on the northern boundary of Sussex and Thomas Paine, whose revolutionary zeal made such an impact on his fellow members of the Headstrong Club at the White Hart, Lewes, in the eighteenth century.

Taking all the trails together, most of the county is covered. Armchair travellers can do the journeys in imagination and so increase their enjoyment of the stories of their favourite authors.

> *You came, and looked, and loved*
> *the view*
> *Long known and loved by me,*
> *Green Sussex fading into blue*
> *With one grey glimpse of sea.*
>
> Alfred Lord Tennyson, who lived
> at Black Down

6

Trail 1

TWO NOVELISTS AND TWO EARLS

H G Wells; Elizabeth von Arnim; Francis, Earl Russell; Bertrand Russell

Locations: Midhurst, Uppark, South Harting; and Telegraph House, North Marden.

Distance: From Midhurst to Uppark, South Harting; then to North Marden and back to Midhurst via Rogate is about twenty five miles.

Map: OS Landranger Sheet 197 (Chichester and the Downs).

Parking: In Midhurst, on east side of North Street there is a large public car park. Uppark has parking for visitors; on Harting Down at North Marden there is a public car park.

Refreshments: There is a restaurant at Uppark. Teas are also available when the chalk garden at Telegraph House is open.

Buildings: After the fire of 1989 Uppark has been fully restored and is open to National Trust members and non-members fom June 1 to October 31, Sunday to Thursday. The exhibition, garden, shop and restaurant open at noon, the house at 1pm. Entry is by timed ticket, the last ones being isued at 5pm. The house closes at 5.30pm. Admissions can be booked in advance by telephoning 01730 825317 Monday to Friday between 9am and noon. Admission charges are: Adults £5, children £2.50 and family tickets £12.50. The gardens of Telegraph House are open this year on June 22 and 23 and July 13 and 14 from 2 to 6pm. Admission is £1.50, children half price. Private visits are welcome between May and August. To make an appointment telephone 01730 825206.

Suggested route: From Midhurst take the A272 west towards Petersfield; turn left at Stedham Common on to the road signposted to Elsted and continue on it to South Harting. For Uppark turn left on to the B2146 and the entrance is on the left and clearly signposted.

7

After visiting Uppark drive back towards South Harting and, before entering the village, turn right on to the B2141 towards Chichester. The second on the left, just before entering North Marden, leads into a car park from which there are splendid views.

Telegraph House is approached by a private drive, over which there is public access only when the garden is open. However, the house can be reached by a footpath. Follow the South Downs Way east, then south along the base of Little Round Down. Where the Way turns sharp left and rejoins the ridge of the Downs, turn half right on to the bridleway, from which the house may be seen. It was originally called Beacon Hill House but the name was changed to Telegraph House as there was at one time a signalling station there – one of a line set up by the Admiralty so messages could be sent between the Fleet at Portsmouth and London. The return from North Marden to Midhurst can be made via South Harting and then to Rogate and back east along A272 to Midhurst.

HERBERT GEORGE WELLS 1866–1946

'MIDHURST has always been a happy place for me. I suppose it rained there at times but all my memories of Midhurst are in sunshine,' writes Wells in his *Experiment in Autobiography,* published in 1934. He was there as a youngster, first in 1881 as apprentice to Mr Cowap in his chemist's shop in Church Hill – an experience on which he drew extensively in *Tono Bungay.* He did not continue this career as the cost of qualifying was beyond his mother's means.

'I was reluctant to abandon this start because I liked the bright little shop . . . and I had taken to Midhurst from the outset. It had been the home of my grandparents, and that gave me a sense of belonging there,' he wrote. 'I know of no country that can compare with West Sussex except the Cotswolds. It had its own colour, a pleasant colour of sunlit sandstone and ironstone and a warm flavour of open country because of the parks and commons and pine woods about it.'

He was at Midhurst again in 1883 for a stint as a pupil teacher at

Uppark, South Harting, where Sarah Wells was housekeeper for thirteen years.

the grammar school. He lodged above the sweetshop next to the Angel Hotel in North Street – it is still there – and wrote about that period of his life in *Love amd Mr Lewisham,* (1900).

At Uppark his mother was housekeeper to the elderly Miss Fetherstonhaugh. Sarah Neal had been born in Midhurst, where her parents had an inn. As a girl she been a ladies' maid at Uppark and married the gardener there, Joseph Wells. The couple left Sussex to begin a difficult, itinerant married life.

It was while they were running a china shop in Bromley, where, at the age of seven, H G went to Mr Morley's Commercial Academy, Joseph Wells broke his leg and could no longer contribute much to the household. To save the family finances Sarah accepted an invitation to return to Uppark as housekeeper to the unmarried lady of the house and when he was there with her H G had the run of the library 'which abounded in bold and enlightening books'.

9

His education wa continued at Midhurst Grammar School, where he went first for lessons in Latin – knowledge of which was necessary for a potential pharmaceutical chemist – and then spent two months as a boarder learning elementary science.

Wells, who worked his own way through the University of London, where he studied under the great biologist, Thomas Huxley, draws heavily on his own life in his realistic novels.

In *The Wheels of Chance* his hero bicycles through the villages of West Sussex in the car-free world of the 1890s; *Kipps* records his days as a draper's assistant at Southsea. His later books were increasingly the vehicles for new ideas about society. They were concerned with improving people's living conditions and embraced socialism, feminism, nationalism, evolutionism and the advancement of science as a means of doing so.

He was the first significant writer of science fiction – and one with a science background. The turn of the century reading public could not get enough of such books as *The Invisible Man*, (1897), *The War of the Worlds*, (1898) and *The Time Machine* (1895). Neither could succeeding generations. They have been continually in print and adapted for film, radio, television and for the stage.

Wells's non fiction was as popular as his fiction. He had an immense success with *A Short History of the World* (1922) for which he enlisted the help of academic friends and of his long-suffering wife, Jane. The book charts mankind's progress through the evolution of the creatures to the casting off of religious superstitions with the advancement of science.

The author was immediately attacked by one of his contemporaries, then with a home in Sussex. Hilaire Belloc was also a prolific writer of histories, but they were not the best of sellers.

In articles in various journals he took issue with what Wells wrote about evolution and did so in such a way that left the author of *A Short History of the World* at a disadvantage and with no satisfactory way of replying.

10

Wells knew many of the literary figures of his time, Indeed he made love to at least two of them – the young Rebecca West, who bore him a son, and Elizabeth von Arnim.

He was also a friend of Henry James and visited him at Rye. Neither really approved of the other's literary works. James, as the elder statesman of letters, disapproved of novels that were based on real experience. He believed they should be constructed with imagination.

Wells on the other hand wondered 'why on earth any man should think it worth while to tell so feeble a story at such length, and with such gloating. When there is so much real life, and when so much needed voicing and changing, how could one sit down to write a made story, with however great a finesse?'

ELIZABETH VON ARNIM 1870-1941

SHE was not born Elizabeth, but she virtually invented herself and her name, rather as did Rebecca West, with whom she shared the favours of H G Wells. Some of her twenty books, including *Mrs Skeffington, Christopher and Columbus* and *Enchanted April*, which was made into an award winning television drama, have been re-published by Virago Press in recent years.

For a part of her long and complicated life she was mistress of Telegraph House, high on the South Downs under the shelter of Beacon Hill near South Harting. Here she was first the lover and then wife of Francis, Earl Russell, older brother of Bertrand, who also comes into the story.

Elizabeth's early life is like a romantic novel too. She was born Mary Annette Beauchamp in Sydney, Australia, the youngest of Henry and Louey Beauchamp's six children. In 1870 the family came to England and her father reluctantly spent money to launch her into society as he had no great expectations of her finding a rich husband. When, while being trailed by her parents round the capitals of Europe, she was wooed and won by Count Henning August von

11

Anim-Schlagenthin, a widower fifteen years her senior, both she and they were rather overwhelmed and not a little apprehensive.

With her marriage May, as she was known to her family, became Countess von Arnim, and it was on the von Arnim estate in Pommerania that she wrote about making a garden in Germany in the English manner. *Elizabeth and Her German Garden* was published, anonymously, in 1898 and gave its author not only literary success but a name.

'Elizabeth', the name she chose as a nom de plume, had a succession of lovers and another husband after her first died. She became a countess for a second time in 1916 when she married Francis, Earl Russell. It was not a happy union. His behaviour was often like that of a spoiled child, perhaps because of his own troubled childhood. He was totally self centred and used his wealth and power to get his own way. If he were thwarted he would pursue those who opposed him with law suits.

Before the First World War he had built Telegraph House in a shallow tree-filled valley below the Bronze Age earthworks of Beacon Hill. It has a rather bleak square tower with large plain windows and Elizabeth called it Bluebeard's castle. In *Vera*, published in 1921 after she had separated from Francis, she described its unprepossessing interior with vengeful accuracy.

The novel's bullying, sadistic 'hero', Edward Wemyss, was, to her circle of friends, a recognisable portrait of her husband. He, like Edward, bullied the household staff sadistically, and bedded a parlourmaid from time to time. He had had two wives, apart from parlourmaids, before he met Elizabeth, who presumably married him to shield her children from the anti-German feeling prevalent in the early years of the war.

Francis thought of suing her for libel over *Vera*, but considered that would have the effect of increasing its sales. Instead he sued the firm engaged to remove Elizabeth's belongings from Telegraph House, on the grounds that they were his property. When the case came to court

Elizabeth was called as a witness and some of the exchanges verged on the farcical. . .

Mr Mould (for Lord Russell): Now, with regard to the hammock. Do you say that you did not give that to Lord Russell?

Lady Russell: Certainly not. It was entirely for my use. It would not have held him.

Francis lost, of course. However divorce could not be contemplated and they remained legally married.

By the time *Vera* was published she was the mistress of a man thirty years her junior and was living in Switzerland. In 1929 she moved to Mougins in the South of France and ten years later went to America where three of her childen were living.

Francis died in 1931 leaving most of his money to a subsequent mistress, and making no reference to Elizabeth in his autobiography. Bertrand Russell became the Earl, having already leased Telegraph House from his brother. There he and his second wife, Dora, founded a school to embody their progressive educational ideas.

Rather like Elizabeth, Dora had been attracted by the Russell authority and intellect. She had been Bertrand Russell's mistress while he was still married to his first wife, Alys; had pursued him to Russia; and then accompanied him to China.

They married when they had children, and partly because of their dislike of conventional boarding schools, decided to run one of their own. They both wrote on social themes, and the logic of their progressive ideas demanded that the basis of children's education be changed.

In 1927 Dora found herself in charge of all the practical details of setting up the school while Bertrand, having decided on the doctrine it should follow, went off to America on a lecture tour. He, following the Russell tradition, had already made love to the principal woman teacher he had engaged.

The regime at Beacon Hill was the opposite of authoritarian. It was 'to provide the child with all kinds of materials, by means of which it

Telegraph House, North Marden.

would find its own way'.

There was emphasis on a nutritious diet, openness on questions of sex, and self-discipline. The aim was to produce self-sufficient adults who would have no need of a rebellious teenage period, or be aware of a generation gap. Naturally there was no physical punishment. Dora Russell gives an account of the school, and the break up of her marriage with Bertrand, in her autobiography *The Tamarisk Tree.*

Bertrand wrote a definitive *A History of Western Philosophy* (1945) which not only consolidated his reputation as a social reformer but gave him a solid financial reward, much of which he used later for social and political causes. In his old age he was in the public eye as an active nuclear disarmer and was arrested in the 1960s when taking part in a sit-down protest in Trafalgar Square.

Trail 2
A WRITER OF CAUTIONARY TALES. . .
Hilaire Belloc 1870–1953

Locations: Slindon, near Arundel and Shipley, near Horsham.

Distance: Slindon to Shipley by the route suggested is about twenty five miles, and the return about eighteen miles.

Maps: OS Landranger sheets 197 (Chichester and the Downs) and 198 (Brighton and the Downs).

Parking: There is roadside parking in Slindon and in Shipley, not far from the windmill.

Refreshments: When Shipley Mill is open, refreshments are available there. The trail passes many of the inns Belloc visited, all of which serve food.

Buildings: Courthill Farm is privately owned and not open to the public; Kingsland at Shipley was the Belloc family home from 1906 and is also not open to the public. The mill has been restored to working order as a memorial to Belloc by the Shipley Mill Charitable Trust, and is open 2–5pm on the first and third Sunday in the month from April to October, and on bank holiday Mondays. Also this year it is open on National Mill Day, May 12; and Shipley Festival, Saturday and Sunday, May 25 and 26. Information line: 01403 730439. Admission charges: Adults £1.50, OAPs £1, children 50p.

Suggested Route: To reach Slindon from Arundel take the A27 Chichester Road from the bypass roundabout. About two and a half miles along turn right into Mill Road which crosses the A29 and leads into the village. Approaching from the west on the A27 turn left on to the A29 opposite the Fontwell public house, take the next left into Park Road and left again when it joins Mill Road. Courthill Farm is on the north western outskirts of the village. Go along Church Hill, past the church which is on the left into the road to Eartham which runs between Slindon College and the Roman Catholic church. It is

15

advisable to park here and cover the rest of the short distance on foot. Take the little road to the right after the college and Courthill Farm house is on the right, a hundred yards or so along. The road leads eventually to Gumber Farm, now owned by the National Trust. Continue the trail by returning to the A29, heading north-east through wooded country, to the Whiteways roundabout. Go across on to the B2139 which drops down into the Arun valley and the little village of Houghton. Here are the George and Dragon and The Bridge, two of the old inns Belloc called at on his 1902 Sussex walk, which he recorded in *The Four Men*. Other hostelries on his route where The Fountain at Ashurst, The Crabtree at Lower Beeding and the Frankland Arms at Washington. The B2139 goes on through Storrington to cross the A24 at the Washington roundabout. Keep straight on eastward, now on the A283, for another five miles or so and turn left on to the B2135 to Ashurst, noticing or calling at The Fountain, and on to West Grinstead. Here, in the churchyard of Our Lady of Consolation and St Francis, is the Belloc family grave, pictured below. Turn right onto the A24 and then left onto the A272 at

Buckbarn crossroads. Here is the The Cat and Fiddle, much frequented by Belloc when it was a pub. About a mile along turn left into Pound Lane to Shipley. To return to the start of the trail, head south for the A24.

HILAIRE BELLOC 1870-1953

BELLOC is a splendidly complex figure – academic historian, staunch Roman Catholic with a romantic nostaglia for the Middle Ages, sailor, traveller, dissenting Liberal MP, poet and debater. He was a tireless walker through Sussex, although born in Paris in 1870, almost within the sound of the gunfire of the Franco-Prussian war.

After the death of his French father, his mother, Madame Bessie Parkes Belloc, who had been converted to the Churh of Rome by a young Sussex clergyman – later to become Cardinal Manning – settled in Slindon. She rented Slindon Cottage, now known as the Dower House, in 1878 and took up residence there with her two children, Joseph Hilaire Pierre and Marie Adelaide. The latter grew up to become Mrs Bellow Lowndes, a writer of detective stories and thrillers, among them *The Lodger* (1913), an imaginary reconstruction of the Jack the Ripper murders which has been filmed three times -- in 1926, 1932 and 1944.

Later the family moved to Gaston Cottage where Madame Belloc lived until her death, except for a few years spent at The Grange. Her grave can been seen in St Richard's churchyard. It was to the Grange that Hilaire Belloc brought his bride to be, the lovely Elodie whom he had courted in California. In February 1905 he returned to Slindon with Elodie and their five childen to live for eighteen months at Courthill Farm.

From there he moved with his family to Kingsland at Shipley, which he came to regard as his home – but one from which he was mostly away. He was always travelling. There was a famous walk from the north of France, through Switzerland and northern Italy described in *The Path to Rome* (1902); endless peregrinations across France and the Pyrenees; even a trip to Russia to look at battlefields; and to the

17

edge of the Sahara to write a history book at breakneck speed. All the time he was away he had a deep longing for Sussex:

> If ever I become a rich man
> Or if ever I grow to be old,
> I will build a house with deep thatch
> To shelter me from the cold,
> And there shall the Sussex songs be sung
> And the story of Sussex told.

> I will hold my house in the high wood
> Within a walk of the sea,
> And the men that were boys when I was a boy
> Shall sit and drink with me.

Belloc was a prolific writer. Not only did he produce some 150 books but he wrote constantly for magazines. This work provided him with a regular income but it was not, apparently,his preferred way of earning a living:

> Would that I had £300,000 invested in some strong security
> A Midland Country House with formal grounds
> A Town House, and a House beside the sea,
> And one in Spain, and one in Normandy,
> And Friends innumerable at my call
> And youth serene - and underneath it all
> One steadfast, passionate flame to nurture me.

> Then would I chuck for good my stinking trade
> Of writing tosh for 1s 6d. a quire !
> And soar like Bellerophon arrayed
> High to the filmy heavens of my desire...
> But that's all over. Here's the world again.
> Bring me the blotter. Fill the fountain pen.

Unfortunately Belloc was not very good at managing his financial affairs. When he had earned well from his military articles in the First World War, he invested heavily in Russian government bonds just before the 1917 revolution and lost the lot.

Much of his frustration arose from just missing a career as an

Courthill Farmhouse, Slindon where Hilaire Belloc, his wife and five children, stayed for eighteen months from February 1905.

Oxford historian. Although a brilliant undergraduate he failed to get a Fellowship at All Souls, probably because of an outspoken expression of dogmatic views, and his early literary career was precarious. His travel books, *A Path to Rome* and *The Four Men*, are regarded as classics but are long out of print. His poems and his many epigrams survive. He first gained fame with his *Bad Child's Book of Beasts* (1896) followed later by *Cautionary Tales* (1907)

Belloc involved himself in politics but was too much of a rebel ever to join a government. Almost alone in his generation he foresaw the equal shortcomings of capitalism and socialism, and the slavery that both exacted from ordinary people.

19

King's Mill, Shipley.

He can be criticised for an obsession with the role of Jews in Western society, but in this he goes little beyond what was common in his time. He had a long decline into old age in the house at Kingsland, Shipley that he bought in 1906. It looks little different today from when he lived there. The adjoining mill, lovingly restored, includes information about his life and work.

Trail 3

AN ARISTOCRATIC OUTSIDER

Wilfrid Scawen Blunt 1840-1922

Locations: Petworth, Dragons Green, Worth, Crawley.

Distance: From Petworth to Worth and back is about sixty miles.

Maps: OS Landranger Sheets 197 (Chichester and the Downs), 198 (Brighton and the Downs) and 187 (Dorking, Reigate and Crawley).

Parking: There is a visitor's car park at Petworth House, pictured above, and parking in Worth Forest on the north side of the Handcross to Turners Hill road just before its junction with the Worth to Balcombe Road.

Refreshments: Light lunches and teas are available at Petworth House. The George and Dragon is just north of the A272, near Newbuildings Place.

21

Buildings: Petworth House, pictured above, is open From April to October daily, except Monday and Friday, from 1 to 5.30pm, last tickets 4.30pm. Admission charges: Adults £4.20, children half price. The park is open all the year round. Forest Lodge, and Newbuildings Place are private houses not open to the public. Crabbet Park is an equestrian centre, but is not otherwise open to the public. Worth Church, which has a memorial to Wilfrid's parents, is open in daylight hours.

Suggested Route: Starting from Petworth where Blunt was born in the magnificent late seventeenth century Petworth House, which stands in a 700 acre deer park, leave by the A272 east to Wisborough Green. Continue on through Billingshurst and, after passing through Coolham, take the second of the two left turnings signposted to

Newbuildings Place, the house in which the poet spent his later years and in the grounds of which he is buried.

22

Crabbet Park, rebuilt in the Queen Anne style in 1872.

Dragons Green. In the village take the right fork into Dragons Green Lane and Newbuildings Place is on the right. Return to the A272 and continue east, crossing the A24 and heading for Cowfold. In the village turn left and head north on the A281 to Lower Beeding. Take the right fork towards Handcross on the A279 and keep straight on through the village. At the end of the High Street take the right fork on to the B2110 and after about one and half miles bear left, still on the B2110 towards Turners Hill. At its T-junction with the B2036 turn left towards Horley. The road passes through Worth Forest and crosses the M23 motorway.

On the left, immediately after the motorway bridge, is Forest Cottage, where Blunt used to stay as a young man. A few hundred yards further on fork right into Street Hill and the next turning on the right is signposted to Worth Church, now among new houses. Return to the B2036, and go north to the next major right turning, signposted to Turners Hill. Follow this road over the motorway again and Crabbet Park Equestrian Centre is approached by a private road immediately on the left. Continue on the road to Turners Hill for about two miles and it leads into the B2210 at a reversed Y-junction just after the church. Turn back right on the road to Handcross and follow the outward route through Cowfold and Billingshurst to Petworth.

> Dear checker-work of woods, the Sussex Weald!
> If a name thrills me yet of things of earth
> That name is thine. How often I have fled
> To thy deep hedgerows and embraced each field
> Each lag, each pasture – fields which gave me birth
> And saw my youth, and which must hold me dead.
>
> From *Love Sonnets of Proteus*

Wilfrid Blunt, poet, author, diplomat and explorer was bitterly opposed to British imperialism and was imprisoned for an inflammatory speech in favour of Home Rule for Ireland. He travelled in the diplomatic service and in a private capacity throughout Europe, the Near East and India and when, in the 1920s, his most interesting prose work, *My Diaries 1888-1914*, was published, it was withdrawn because of the secrets of British diplomacy it revealed.

He had a fascinating and turbulent life. He was born the second son of a wealthy squire who owned about 4,000 acres of north Sussex, and he inherited the lot in 1867 when his elder brother died.

He was born at Petworth House where his aunt, the wife of Colonel George Wyndham, who became the first Lord Leconfield, lived. The infant Wilfrid, already fatherless, was for a time at Petworth Old Rectory, and would no doubt have been taken to Petworth House to play with his Wyndham cousins.

His widowed mother, having become a Roman Catholic – she was converted by the same Sussex clergyman who influenced the mother of Hilaire Belloc to turn to Rome – took her children to live in France and Italy.

Wilfrid was educated at Roman Catholic schools and was never part of the public schools' Old Boy network. However he went into the diplomatic service and it was during his early years serving his country in this capacity that he wrote many of the poems which appeared in his *Collected Poems*, published when he was an old man.

He married the granddaughter of Byron, Lady Annabel Noel. They travelled – but that is an understatement. Blunt already knew Europe, and with his wife he explored Arabia, and formed a passion for Arab horses and the romance of the desert. They went on to India, where, having chatted with his friend the Viceroy and observed the poverty outside the Viceregal walls, he wrote an attack on the British policy in India which distressed his establishment friends.

Home again, he and his wife, acting as their own architects, rebuilt Crabbet Park in Queen Anne style and there they bred Arab horses.

He invited his literary and political friends down to an annual 'occasion' in which they had to compete in poetry and at lawn tennis, then in its infancy as a country house game. He also travelled throughout England with horses and a wagon, sometimes camping, sometimes staying with friends.

All the time he poured out poems, pamphlets, letters to *The Times*, letters to Government ministers and kept voluminous diaries.

Wilfrid Blunt in Diplomatic Corps uniform

In these he gives a rundown of the candidates in the Poet Laureate stakes following the death of Tennyson; describes the 'daubs' of the first Post-Impressionist Exhibition in 1911, which revealed the works of Gauguin and others to a shocked English public; and mourns the passing of his great friend, William Morris.

25

In his poem The Wind and the Whirlwind, he rages against what he sees as the cruelties of the British Empire. Here are a few of the many verses:

> Thou sellest the sad nations to their ruin
> What hast thou bought? The child within the womb,
> The son of him who thou slayest to thy hurting
> Shall answer thee "An Empire for thy tomb"...
>
> Thou hast joined house to house for thy perdition
> Thou hast done evil in the name of right.
> Thou hast made bitter sweet and the sweet bitter
> And called light darkness and the darkness light.
>
> The Empire thou hast built shall be divided.
> Thou shalt be weighed in thine own balances
> Of usury to peoples and to princes
> And be found wanting by the world and these.

Blunt eventually moved to Newbuildings Place, first leasing Crabbet Park and later handing it over to his wife, from whom he had separated, partly over disagreements about money and partly over his many women friends.

He also owned a cottage in Worth Forest and built another house, now demolished, not far away from it. He spent the winters in Egypt where he brooded on the machinations of the great powers as they jostled for territory in Africa and the Middle East.

Blunt, who had embraced Islam when in Arabia, became a Roman Catholic shortly before he died. In his will, made years before, he had directed that verses from the Koran should be read over his grave in the woods at Newbuildings Place. As he had not changed it he was buried with both Christian and Islamic rites.

Trail 4

A WALK IN POOH BEAR COUNTRY

A A Milne 1882–1956 and Christopher Robin Milne 1920–

Location: In and around Ashdown Forest, south of Hartfield.

Distance: Once in the Hartfield area distances are short and best covered on foot. There are two walks – the first of about three miles, the second about two.

Map: OS Landranger sheet 188 (Maidstone and the Weald of Kent).

Parking: Ashdown Forest is well supplied with free public car parks. There is roadside parking in Hartfield.

Suggested route: Most of the sites – the Pooh Bridge, Galleons Lap, Hundred Acre Wood and Cotchford Farm, the home of A A Milne

Cotchford Farm, Hartfield, where A A Milne wrote the tales that made him famous.

27

and Christopher Robin – can really only be reached on foot. The area is part of Ashdown Forest and can be approached from the north on the B2026 then south from Hartfield or from the A264 East Grinstead to Tunbridge Wells road.

The approach from the south is on the A22 Eastbourne to London road. From it the B2026 is a right fork, signposted Hartfield, between Nutley and Maresfield. Alternatively, just north of Nutley on the A22, heading for East Grinstead, turn right to the A26 and Tunbridge Wells amd this road joins the B2026. Head for the car park four miles south of Hartfield, near the road branching off the B2026 to Newbridge and Forest Row.

This is the 'Top of the Forest'. From the car park a footpath leads north a few hundred yards to Gills Lap – Galleons Lap in the Pooh stories – or a round walk of about two miles can take one in an anti-clockwise direction through pleasant wooded paths and over heathy slopes with wide views. To the north east is Hundred Acre Wood where Owl's tree was a great beech, long since gone in a storm.

A second starting point for exploration is the car park in Possingford Wood. From the top of the forest take the B2026 north in the direction of Hartfield and it is less than a couple of miles to a left turn to Chuck Hatch. A short way on the right there is a car park in the woods. A little further along that road a bridle path heads off to the right. It is often muddy but it leads eventually to the stream spanned by the bridge from which Pook sticks was played.

There is an alternative path through the woods from the car park, coming out again on the road shortly before the bridle path. The latter is now signposted Pooh Bridge. By keeping on this track as it bears right, eventually rejoining the B2026, Cotchford Farm can be seen on the right. It is a private house and not open to the public.

In Hartfield is the sweetshop to which the real Christopher Robin was taken on a donkey to buy his sweets. It is still there, packed with Winnie the Pooh memorabilia. The whole Ashdown Forest area is good rambling country, offering wide views over the Weald of Sussex.

A A Milne and his son, Christopher Robin, painted by Howard Coster, 1926.
Photo: National Portrait Gallery.

The Enchanted Place from where ' they could see the whole world spead out until it reached the sky'.

'They walked on, thinking of This and That, and by-and-by they came to an enchanted place on the Top of the Forest called Galleons Lap, which is sixty-something trees in a circle; and Christopher Robin knew that it was enchanted because nobody had ever been able to count whether it was sixty three or sixty four . . .'

This trail is a rather special one for the devotees of the Christopher Robin stories. It has a landscape with literary associations in which it is possible to walk to the Top of the Forest; find the North Pole with Christopher Robin and Pooh; see Hundred Acre Wood, where Owl lived; and have a game of Pooh sticks on Pooh Bridge.

The same countryside can be explored in the company of the real Christopher Robin, now living in Devonshire. He has relived his childhood in his book, *Enchanted Places*, and it includes an extremely helpful map.

So what about A A Milne – what sort of man was he? His father

30

was a headmaster, and as a young man Alan had a brilliant career as assistant editor of Punch. He married a wife who laughed at his jokes. From the house in London where Christopher Robin was born in 1920, the couple moved to Sussex in 1925.

Among the many stories, plays and novels he wrote, A A Milne's reputation, as he realised ruefully before he died, rested on four short books, quickly written and not much regarded by their author at the time. *When We Were Very Young* (1924) and *Now We Are Six* (1927) are collections of verse for children, *Winnie the Pooh* (1926) and *The House at Pooh Corner* (1928) have Pooh, a toy bear, as their hero.

They were originally intended be read in the family circle rather than for publication but they appeared at a time his books for adults and his plays were going out of fashion and brought him instant success. But they also became a burden to him – as they did to his son. Like so many other authors he had a growing sense of failure because

Pooh Bridge, built in 1907 and rebuilt some sixteens year ago by East Sussex County Council.

31

his serious work seemed so little regarded and his lighter storeis and verse widely appreciated. He complained bitterly of a review in which the hero of his play was described as 'just Christopher Robin grown up'.

'Even when I stop writing about children I shall insist on writing about people who were children once', he said.

The real Christopher Robin also showed resentment at becoming a character in his father's tales. This he tried to exorcise in his three books of autobiography, of which *Enchanted Places* is the first.

'My father had got to where he was by climbing upon my infant shoulders. . . he had filched from me my good name and left me with nothing but the empty fame of being his son.' That is how C R Milne thought as a young man in 1947.

In the succeeding volumes of his autobiography, *The Path Through the Wood* and *The Hollow on the Hill,* Christopher Robin Milne tells very movingly how he came out from the shadow of his childhood and was able to accept the part his father had written for him. He could even manage, just, to shake hands with children whose doting parents brought them to his Dartmouth bookshop just in order to say: 'There, now you have shaken hands with the real Christopher Robin'.

Trail 5

THE BLOOMSBURY GROUP – AND OTHER WRITERS AT RODMELL

Virginia and Leonard Woolf, Clive Bell, John Maynard Keynes. Beachcomber and friends.

Locations: Rodmell, between Lewes and Newhaven; Charleston and Tilton, near Firle.

Distances: Newhaven to Rodmell is about three and a half miles; Rodmell to Charleston, via Lewes about nine and a half miles; Charleston back to Newhaven via Berwick and Alfriston is about eleven and a half miles.

Maps: OS Landranger Sheets 198 (Brighton and the Downs) and 199 (Eastbourne and Hastings).

Parking: There is roadside parking at Rodmell as well as a National Trust car park. Parking at Charleston is limited to the car park for visitors to the house.

Refreshments: The Abergavenny Arms in Rodmell. On the main A27 near Charleston is Middle Farm Shop for light lunches and teas.

Buildings: Monk's House, Rodmell is owned by the National Trust (tel: 01372 453401) and there is a custodian in residence. It is open Wednesday and Saturday afternoons from 2pm from April 1 to the end of October. Charleston Farmhouse, which has its own Trust, (tel: 01323 811265 for visitor information) is open from 2 to 6pm Wednesdays to Sundays and bank holiday Mondays from April to the end of October; and from 11am Wednesday to Saturday from the second week in July to the end of August. In November and December selected rooms can be viewed at a reduced charge on Saturday and Sunday between 2pm and 5pm. Tilton is privately owned and not open to the public, nor are Hilltop Farm and Charnes Cottage, Rodmell.

Suggested Route: From Newhaven take the C7 road north signposted to Piddinghoe, Southease and Kingston. At Rodmell, where there are three properties with literary associations, turn right into the main street for Monk's House and Charnes Cottage, which are separated one from the other, by the path leading to the church. Hill Top Farm is at the top of a lane leading off the main road in the opposite direction from the street in which Monk's House stands. Roadside parking is possible a little way up this lane, after which there is footpath access only.

After Rodmell continue north to Lewes where there is much of historical and architectural interest. Leave the town on the A27 going east through the tunnel. Follow this main road, passing the right turn to Firle, and the narrow turning to Charleston Farmhouse is on the right about two miles further on. Nearby, close to the footpath leading east and then south from Charleston Farmhouse, is Tilton Farm. From Charleston, return to the A27, turn right and right again at the Drusillas roundabout to return to Newhaven via Alfriston and Seaford.

VIRGINIA WOOLF 1884-1941

THERE was a marked contrast between Rodmell's literary communities in the between-the-wars period. On the one hand there was a group of beer-drinking, cricket-playing poets, novelists and writers with a rumbustious love of the Sussex countryside. On the other there was Virginia Woolf, a woman of genius whose books are known for their delicacy and sensitivity of style and subtle evocation of place and mood.

Leonard and Virginia Woolf came to Monk's House in 1919, and until Virginia's death in 1941 spent many weeks and week-ends there, especially in the summer months.

Virginia, and her sister Vanessa, where brought up in an atmosphere of literature and learning in the home of their father Sir Leslie Stephen. After his death writers and artists who had been friends at Cambridge would meet at the salon the sisters held at 46 Gordon

Square to talk and exchange and develop their ideas. So began the Bloomsbury Group. Vanessa married one of its members – the art and literary critic, Clive Bell; Virginia another – Leonard Woolf, a writer on politics and economics.

Virginia had long periods of depression, sometimes related to the progress being made on her current book. After her nervous breakdown in 1912, the year they were married, Leonard took on the task of guarding his wife from any stresses that could affect her frail mental health. When she was well she was the life and soul of the party – and of Bloomsbury in the country.

Virginia Woolf
Photo: National Portrait Gallery

Monks House was a primitive retreat to start with. It still looks cold, as it was to many of the guests who stayed there, and Virginia's bedroom is rather like a cell.

There were servants, of course, and gardeners and greenhouses. When she had given her staff their instructions each morning Virginia would retire to her writing room – a wooden shed at the end of the garden. Even in the depths of winter she would work there and it is possible to picture her, on a cold November in 1940, with her Bloomsbury house now bombed, looking out over the frost covered fields of the Ouse valley and to the Downs beyond, as she wrote her last book *Between The Acts*. Its theme is the continuity of English history – and a belief in the future.

Contemporary opinion of her novels considered them strange and experimental. The streams of the inner thoughts of the characters made them so different from the real life plots of Galsworthy or Bennett, whom she criticised sternly. She was even more caustic in her diaries about the young writers on her doorstep – particularly as they

Monks House, Rodmell and, below, Charnes Cottage were Edward Shanks lived.

left empty beer bottles on it. She found the poet, Edward Shanks was living almost too close for comfort. His cottage could be seen from her sitting room but she had nothing to do with him, and dismissed him as 'of boneless mind'. Bushes have now grown up between the houses so the one cannot be easily seen from the other.

Having found her retreat at Rodmell Virginia was angry that others had found it too. On 31 August 1920 she recorded in her diary how she sat in her meadow – now an extension of the garden where visitors can wander – and watched John Squire and Siegfried Sassoon play cricket: 'The last people I wished to see . . . Somehow that the Downs should be seen by cultivated eyes spoils them to me'.

About that time she tried to persuade Leonard to sell and move elsewhere. But they stayed.

They had their own guests at weekends. In Virginia's writing room are splendid sepia photographs of E M Forster and T S Eliot at Monks House in the full formality of waistcoats and hats – 'in his four-piece suit', Virginia used to say, mocking Eliot's smartness.

Vita Sackville-West – model for the time travelling, gender changing subject of *Orlando: A Biography* (1928) – and her husband, Harold Nicholson would come over from Sissinghurst, the composer Ethel Smyth was a frequent visitor, as was John Lehmann who was to work with Leonard and Virginia at the Hogarth Press from 1931 to 1946. On one occasion even John Squire was invited. He was, after all, the editor of the *London Mercury* and paid good money for literary work.

Money was never too plentiful at Monks House and Virginia made the point in *A Room of One's Own* (1929) that 'one' needed £500 to set up as an independent writer.

In the early years of the war Virginia's frail mental health failed again. On a cold March day in 1941 she walked out of Monk's House and through the fields that lead to the river. . . Some three weeks later her drowned body was recovered from the Ouse and, at an inquest at Newhaven, the East Sussex Coroner recorded a verdict of 'suicide while the balance of the mind was disturbed'.

Charleston Farmhouse, West Firle

O stalwart SUSSEX postman, who is
Delivering the post from LEWES
Cycle apace to CHARLESTON, FIRLE,
While knitting at your plain and purl,
Deliver there to good CLIVE BELL,
(You know the man, you know him well,
He plays the virginals and spinet),
This note - there's almost nothing in it.

THIS is T S Eliot addressing an envelope to his friend, Clive Bell, a writer among artists at Charleston. The paintings of his wife, Vanessa, and of Duncan Grant cover almost every surface at the farmhouse.

In *Old Friends,* published in 1956, Clive Bell's genial collection of essays about Eliot and his contemporaries, he quotes the verse and adds: 'This pleasantry gave satisfaction to the postman invoked. He considered it "clever". He was not quite sure about the "spinet", but knew that I was fond of a bit of shooting: it was not true about the "virginals" he hoped.'

Clive Bell combined a Bloomsbury concern with matters of intellect and of art with the background of a sporting country gentleman, and the money to go with it. He was one of the circle of Cambridge undergraduates whom Virginia and her sister Vanessa met through their brother Thoby.

Their marriage was unconventional but relaxed. Vanessa tolerated Clive's mistress, Mary Hutchinson, while she lived contentedly with the artist, Duncan Grant, who had been the youthful lover of Maynard Keynes. They divided their time between Gordon Square in Bloomsbury and Charleston, and Clive provided the money.

Having helped Roger Fry stage the Post-Impressionists Exhibition that so outraged London society, he wrote a book simply entitled *Art*. In it he preaches the doctrine that what an observer sees in a picture is significant form – that is, the pattern of colour and lines rather than the stories in paint that Victorians loved.

He went on to write *Civilization*, in which he explained that the high points of civilization, if it is to have any real meaning, are periods when at least a privileged minority of society is truly able to appreciate art and good style, rather than comfort or riches. This extract sums up his argument:

'If teachers could make ordinary boys and girls realise that the delight of being alone in a bedsitting room with an alert and well-stocked mind and a book is greater than owning yachts and race-horses, and that the thrill of a great picture or a quartet by Mozart is keener than the first sip of a glass of champagne . . . the teachers would have solved the central problem of humanity . . . the only people who possess the key to this palace of pleasures are those who know how to value art and thought for their own sakes, and knowledge as an instrument of culture.'

Tilton

JOHN MAYNARD KEYNES 1883-1946

KEYNES came into the Bloomsbury circle in the same way as Bell – as a clever undergraduate with a shared belief in the values put forward by Cambridge professor of philosophy, G E Moore.

Keynes fixed his penetrating mind, with the Bloomsbury Group's scorn of Victorian convention, on economics. He wore himself out, some say, trying to stop a repetition of the economic follies that had produced the slumps and unemployment of the between the wars years.

He spent his life first in the Treasury and later as a financial adviser to governments and as a Fellow of King's College, Cambridge. His book, *The Economic Consequences of the Peace,* made him a worldwide reputation and he became rich by speculating on the Stock Exchange as well as by writing. In his personal financial dealings he was not infallible and twice lost all his money.

As a young man he was homosexual and surprised and alarmed his friends by wooing and marrying, in 1925, an exiled Russian ballerina, Lydia Lopokova. She was a dancer in Diaghilev's Ballets Russe, a company ecstatically received by the intelligentsia in London and other European capitals before and after the First World War.

Vanessa Bell's reaction was immediate and forthright. She wrote to Maynard: 'As for Loppi, don't marry her. . . Clive says he thinks it impossible for any one of us – you, he, I, Duncan – to introduce a new wife or husband into the existing circle for more than a week at a time. We feel that no one can come into the sort of intimate society we have without altering it.'

She was right. Marriage altered Maynard's relationship with the household at Charleston. At one time he had his own room there, and would come down at weekends with a pile of government papers and with letters to write. Having worked through these with incredible speed, he would relax by taking a broken table knife and digging the weeds out of the garden path. In the evenings they would all settle down together to read and to talk.

This all changed. Keynes took a lease of Tilton Farm, just a few hundred yards away, and spent weekends and summers there. Visits to Charleston were few, except for Christmas and birthdays. He added a loggia and library at the south end of the house and there he wrote his epoch-making testament, *The General Theory of Employment, Interest and Money,* which was published in 1936.

At Tilton there were also ballet rehearsals and other entertainments and Keynes developed an interest in the land, acquired the rest of the farm and raised a herd of pigs.

Among his colleagues Keynes was known as a clear communicator. Clive Bell, not over generous with his praise, says of him: 'If asked to explain some technical business, which to the amateur seemed incomprehensible almost, he would with good humoured ease make the matter appear so simple that one knew not whether to be more amazed at his intelligence or one's own stupidity.'

BEACHCOMBER AND FRIENDS

JOHN Cameron Audrieu Bingham Michael Morton was a young man who, after Harrow, gained entrance to Worcester College, Oxford but left after only a year as his father had lost all his money and was seriously ill.

He survived the trauma of the trenches in the First World War to publish a novel about his experiences, *The Barber of Putney*, and through the aid of an uncle, got a job on the *Sunday Express*. He switched to the *Daily Express* when the founder of its Beachcomber column, D B Wyndham Lewis, left to join the *Daily Mail*.

Johnny Morton seems to have had a free hand with the column and a stream of gentle satire and surreal humour flowed from his pen for the next fifty years. He produced a set of English characters that were household names for a time and were transferred to radio and television. There is Dr Smart-Aleck the criminal headmaster, Captain Foulenough the professional cad, Mr Justice Cocklecarrot, whose court totters between legal quibble and total daftness as real courts all too often do, and many more. He mocked the pretensions of high society, of new religions, and journalistic hypocrisy.

Not everyone appreciated the humour. George Orwell implied that Beachcomber lacked patriotism for pouring scorn on 'tea, cricket, Wordsworth, kindness to animals, Nelson and what not'.

Admittedly, Morton followed his master, Hilaire Belloc, as a Catholic apologist, and as one always ready to jibe at modern art or science. But it is hard not to be captivated by Mrs McGurgle, the seaside landlady, and the other splendid characters he created. Or not to laugh with the writer when, finding his column had not the requisite number of words, added:

'NEWS ITEM: At three o'clock yesterday afternoon there was a sharp shower of green Chartreuse over South Croydon.' He received several letters from people who said that they had been in South Croydon at the time and had noticed no such shower.

Morton spent half his time in London, where he shared a flat with

Edward Shanks, an assistant editor on the *London Mercury*, and the other half in the cottage he bought in Rodmell. He was introduced to the village by Shanks, who lived in Charnes Cottage, just across the church footpath from Monks House.

Murray Allison, a wealthy Australian friend of John Squire and a backer of magazines, kept open house for aspiring poets and writers at Hilltop Farm at the western end of the village. He would host the visits of literary cricket teams to play the village team on the pitch next to the church. Among the famous poets who came to Rodmell for the cricket and the company were Edmund Blunden and war poet and autobiographer, Siegfried Sassoon.

The cricket, and the pitch by St Peter's Church, are described by another member of the group, A G Macdonnell, in his classic *England, Their England*.

This happy account of literary life between the wars contains thinly-disguised portraits of Morton, Peter Belloc and Sir John Squire. In it is described the quintessential village cricket match in which the batsmen have to be lured out of the pub to play, and the village black-smith makes the earth tremble as he runs up to bowl.

Trail 6

THE ROAD TO 1984
George Orwell 1903-1974; Cyril Connolly 1903-1950

Locations: Eastbourne and Blackboys.

Distance: From Eastbourne seafront to Tickerage Mill by the route suggested is about twenty eight miles, and the return via Uckfield and the A22 about twenty one miles miles.

Map: OS Landranger Sheet 199 (Eastbourne and Hastings).

Parking: Kerbside parking in St John's Road and Summerdown Road, Eastbourne. Roadside parking near the turning to Tickerage Mill on Blackboys to Framfield Road.

Refreshments: The Blackboys Inn, Blackboys.

Buildings: 48 St John's Road and Tickerage Mill are private houses not open to the public; on the site of St Cyprian's School there are now houses and playing fields.

Suggested route: From Eastbourne seafront, past the Wish Tower going towards Beachy Head, take the right fork up St John's Road to see, on the right, No 28 – the last home of Cyril Connolly. Go on to the junction with Meads Road and turn right, back towards Eastbourne town centre. At the bottom of the hill turn left into Compton Place Road, then left into Paradise Drive and right into Summerdown Road. No 67 is the site of St Cyprian's School. St Cyprians Lodge stands at the old entrance gates to No 67. Continue north to the traffic lights at the end of Summerdown Road and turn left on to the A259 heading towards Brighton.

For a scenic route drive into the Cuckmere Valley and turn right at the bottom of Exceat hill towards Litlington and on through Alfriston to join the A27 at the Berwick roundabout. Go straight across towards Berwick station, heading for Lower Dicker and the

44

A22. Turn left on the A22, towards London, and at the Halland roundabout turn right for Blackboys. In the village turn left immediately after the Blackboys Inn and then left again on to the B2102 to Framfield. Just on the edge of Blackboys village is Tickerage Lane. Roadside parking is just possible – either on the main road or outside the houses at the top of Tickerage Lane. There is a public path down to Tickerage Mill, but the road is private. The path leads down past the mill and across to fields the other side, from which the mill pond can be seen. From Framfield roads lead direct or via Uckfield to the A22 for the return to Eastbourne.

'I HAD two friends – George Orwell and Cecil Beaton,' wrote Cyril Connolly. 'I was a stage rebel, Orwell a true one. Tall, pale, and with supercilious voice, he was one of those boys who seem born old. He saw through St Cyprian's, despised its headmaster, but was invaluable to them as scholarship fodder. We often walked together over the Downs in our green jerseys and our corduroy breeches discussing literature.'

There they are, two boys aged about twelve, discussing each other's poetry in the intervals between cold baths, games and Latin. Both are conscious that their parents are not able to pay full fees, but they both win scholarships to Eton.

George Orwell, born Eric Blair, was already disillusioned with the tales of Empire on which schoolboys were fed. As an adult he headed for low life and reported on the living conditions of the poor in Paris, London or Wigan. His hatred of the ruling classes, to which he could have belonged, was tempered by a gritty down to earth patriotism.

Both Cyril and Eric, in later life, wrote of their Eastbourne schooldays with deep dislike. Orwell's piece, *Such, Such Were the Joys,* was so fierce that it was not published until both he and the formidable survivor of St Cyprian's, the headmaster's wife, were dead.

In later life Connolly softened his view of the school, and other old boys have rallied round to describe its virtues. It was burned down one Sunday in May 1939, and its site at 67 Summerdown Road has been considerably redeveloped.

Eastbourne Central Library has an archive on the school, as well as an extended account of it in the Twenties by another famous old boy, the golfer Henry Longhurst.

The two literary lives took different courses, but their paths crossed occasionally. George Orwell went to Burma as a policeman, and confirmed his dislike of Empire. Then struggling to support himself as a writer, he worked as a waiter in Paris and became a tramp in England, experiences that resulted in the publication in 1933 of *Down and Out in Paris and London.*

St Cyprian's Lodge is at the entrance to the site of the school.

Cyril Connolly aspired to the high life, lamenting that he never had quite enough money and leisure to write that great masterpiece that he knew must be inside him. Both he and Orwell risked their lives in the Spanish Civil War.

Connolly travelled constantly in inter-war Europe, and pined for it during the last war. In blitz torn London he amazingly brought out a new and successful literary magazine, *Horizon,* which gave voice to the then struggling but later famous writers of the time.

Evelyn Waugh gives a wicked little cameo of him as Everard Spruce with his coterie of attendant women in the last book of his wartime trilogy, *Unconditional Surrender.*

Aside from his entertaining books of literary criticism, Connolly left an elegant Thirties novel, *The Rock Pool,* plus an account of his boyhood in *Enemies of Promise* and a collection of sayings – his own and other people's – entitled *The Unquiet Grave*. This includes the epigram that he composed for his own dismay: `The true function of a writer is to produce a masterpiece and no other task is of any consequence'. Orwell, almost unknown until the end of his life, met that demand.

In those uneasy war years, Connolly came across Orwell again, and indeed published articles by him in *Horizon*. Naturally each has written about the other, usually in book reviews.

Here is Connolly on Orwell:
'He couldn't blow his nose without moralising on the state of the handkerchief industry'.

And here is Orwell on Connolly, about his book *The Unquiet Grave*:
'A cry of despair from the rentier who feels he has no right to exist, but who also feels he is a finer animal than the proletarian'.

Their friendship was not close, but they had one important connection – Sonia Brownell. While Connolly thought great thoughts about literature and wrote pieces for his magazine, the hard work of getting the other contributions and putting the magazine together devolved on a group of devoted women. Of these Sonia became increasingly the most effective editor. She met Orwell, whose first wife had died tragically, and married him shortly before his death from tuberculosis. Thereafter she assiduously edited and arranged for the re-publishing of his many essays and articles.

There is anoher connection between the two In his masterpiece, *1984*, Orwell gives an ironic description of a fantastic totalitarian state, where every thought of every citizen is controlled, where all the assumptions of society are reversed, where the Ministry of Truth means the generation of lies, where people are brainwashed until they are grateful for the degradation they have been forced into.

Connolly had written, in the jokey style he sometimes used as a holiday from his high seriousness, a short piece back in 1938, called *Year Nine*. In it the narrator, who works in the censor's department of a parody of a totalitarian state, is found guilty of liking degenerate art

Tickerage Mill, Blackboys, Connolly's first retreat in Sussex and, below, his last home in the county - 48 St Johns Road, Eastbourne

and - expressing gratitude to the Leader - is sentenced to torture and death. The setting and the coined words 'Leaderday', and 'common-meal' are echoed in *1984*. Did Orwell know the piece, and did it sow in him seeds that grew into a grimmer and fuller version?

After the war Connolly grew tired of *Horizon* and his love life fell apart again - it did so continually. In the Forties he had been given the use of a retreat in Sussex, Tickerage Mill. This is how he describes it in *The Unquiet Grave:*

'The mill where I sometimes stay provides another cure for angst; the red lane down through the Spanish chestnut wood, the apple trees on the lawn, the bees in the roof, the geese on the pond, the black sunlit marsh marigolds, the wood fires crackling in the low bedrooms, the creak of the cellar door, and the recurrent monotonies of the silver whispering weir - what could be more womb like or reassuring? Yet always the anxious owner is flying from it as from the scene of a crime.'

The owner was Dick Wyndham, who filled the mill with parties before the war, except when he was away on photographic expeditions abroad. Wyndham was killed in 1948 when he was a correspondent in Jerusalem, and Tickerage was sold.

By the late Fifties, Connolly was at Bushey Farm, on Lord Gage's Firle estate, not far from Charleston. Later on, still hoping to write a great work, but in fact spending his energies on reviewing, he is drawn to Sussex again. In *Confessions of a House-Hunter* he describes his afternoons in 'Folksbourne' inspecting turreted mansions with soaring gables.

His agent saw him through 'several courtships all ending in disillusion culminating in that of a large Edwardian battlecruiser moored on the edge of a State forest, a Forsyte home 400 feet above sea level'.

He settled in a large Eastbourne house - 48 St John's Road - with a new wife, his third, and children late in life.

Trail 7

FROM THE OUTPOSTS OF EMPIRE

Sir Henry Rider Haggard 1856-1925. Rudyard Kipling 1865-1936

Locations: St Leonards-on-Sea and Burwash.

Distance: From St Leonards to Batemans at Burwash and back to Hastings is a distance of about thirty six miles.

Map: OS Landranger Sheet 199 (Eastbourne and Hastings).

Parking: On St Leonards sea front. Batemans has its own car park for visitors.

Refreshments: Batemans has a restaurant open at the same hours as the house and gardens.

Buildings: North Lodge is private, and not open to the public. Bateman's is owned by The National Trust and is open from April to October every day except Thursday and Friday, 11am to 6 pm.

Suggested Route: A suitable starting point is Maze Hill, St Leonards where, at his brother's house, North Lodge, Sir Henry Rider Haggard stayed on many occasions. The house, which is not open to the public, is at the north end of St Leonards Gardens - just a short distance from the seafront behind the Royal Victoria Hotel. Ideally, park on the front and walk clockwise round St Leonards Gardens or, better still, walk through them Maze Hill circles the gardens and goes north under the gatehouse style building that is North Lodge. It was built in 1830 and a blue plaque records Rider Haggard's occupation of it.

From this point the easiest way out of town is to continue along Upper Maze Hill into Sedlescombe Road South to its roundabout junction with the A21. At the roundabout take the first left, B2159, to Battle. From the roundabout at the end of Battle High Street take the second left fork - the first leads into a shopping complex - and a mile and a half along it, on an awkward left hand bend, take the right fork signposted to Heathfield Road. Continue on this road, it is the B2096, through hilly, wooded country for about three miles to Darwell Hole. Here turn right to Brightling, continue through the village and bear right about a mile further on, towards Burwash. The road runs up over a ridge, with splendid views on all sides, and descends sharply to the valley of the little River Dudwell, at which point there is a narrow left turn leading to Kipling's home, Batemans. The signposts take motorists on the wider roads round the other three sides of a square into Burwash and down the road leading to the house.

For a different route back to St Leonards, drive north from Batemans to Burwash village and turn right along the A265. This joins the A21 Hastings to London road at Hurst Green, passing through Robertsbridge on its way.

North Lodge, St Leonards, where Rider Haggard spent many winters.

51

BOTH Rider Haggard and Rudyard Kipling were associated with stirring tales of the Empire – in which they fervently believed – and they became friends towards the end of their lives.

To avoid the fogs of London and the cold winds of Norfolk, the county which was his home, Haggard spent the winters, in his later years, at his brother's house in St Leonards. Kipling used to visit him in his half of North Lodger and no doubt they would talk about their experiences in India and Africa and perhaps bemoan the decay, as they saw it, of the Imperial ideal.

Their lives illustrate differences between the British in Africa and the British in India when Victoria was queen. Rider Haggard went as a young man to southern Africa, a place where the scattered indigenous inhabitants were treated as mere adjuncts to a life of hunting and diamond mining in the wide empty spaces. Admittedly he served on government commissions for agriculture but much of his work would have been for the white man's benefit as this was colonial territory.

His years in government service in Africa provided the background for the adventure stories which he wrote when he returned to England and married a Norfolk heiress.

His most effective tales of mystery and deeds of heroism on the Dark Continent – *King Solomon's Mines* (1885), *Allan Quartermain* (1887), *She* and its sequel, *Ayesha*, were among the best sellers of their day. The first three were made into highly successful films. Their author was knighted in 1912.

Rudyard Kipling, by contrast, was born in Bombay, the son of a minor English public servant. As a young man he returned to write about life in British ruled India as a reporter on the *Civil and Military Gazette* at Lahore. The verses in *Departmental Ditties* and many stories in *Plain Tales from the Hills* and *Soldiers Three* were written originally for the *Gazette* and the famous tale, *The Man Who Would Be King*, was among those he produced as editor of the *Allahabad Pioneer* in his last two years in India.

He returned to England in 1889 to great success. His Indian books

Batemans, Burwash, where Rudyard Kipling's study is as it was when he wrote his stories there.

had all been republished and he followed them up with *Barrack Room Ballads*, a collection of poems that included *Gunga Din, Tommy* and *Mandalay.*

In 1892 he collaborated with American Woolcott Balestier in writing *The Naulklakha* – and married his co-author's sister, Caroline. The coupled settled on her family's estate in Vermont and there Kipling published *The Jungle Book*; its sequel *The Second Jungle Book*; *The Seven Seas* and *Captains Courageous*. They returned to England and settled in Sussex, first at Rottingdean, then moving in 1902 to Batemans.

The house, left to The National Trust in 1940 by his widow with the request that Kipling's study should remain undisturbed, is a memorial to the first English writer to be awarded the Nobel Prize. And it is a memorial that can be visited. The estate of some 300 acres is surrounded by scenery that inspired the tales he tells in *Puck of Pook's Hill* and *Rewards and Fairies*.

In his newfound love, the motor car, Kipling was able to explore the county which had cast its spell upon him and whose scenery and spirit transformed most of his later work. He had travelled the world but it was to Sussex he wrote this anthem:

> God gave all men all earth to love,
> But, since our hearts are small,
> Ordained for each one spot should prove
> Beloved over all ...
> Each to his choice and I rejoice
> The lot has fallen to me
> A fair land, a fair land
> Yea Sussex by the Sea.
>
> No tender-hearted garden crowns,
> No bosomed woods adorn
> Our blunt, bow-headed, whale-backed Downs,
> But gnarled and writhen thorn -
> Bare slopes where chasing shadows skim,
> And, through the gaps revealed,
> Belt upon belt, the wooded, dim,
> Blue goodness of the Weald.

Trail 8

WRITERS OF RYE

Henry James; E F Benson.; Sheila Kaye-Smith

Location: Rye, Playden and Horns Cross.

Distance: The suggested route from Rye to Playden, Horns Cross and back covers about fifteen miles.

Maps: Landranger Sheets 189 (Ashford) and 199 (Eastbourne and Hastings).

Parking: There are three public car parks, clearly signed, on the left hand side of Wish St/Cinque Ports Street/Tower Street which skirts the bottom of the hill on which the Ancient Port of Rye stands. At Point Hill, Playden, there is only roadside parking. Visitors to the church at Doucegrove can park there.

Buildings: Lamb House, owned first by Henry James and later by E F Benson, is a National Trust property and is open on Wednesday and Saturday between 2pm and 6pm from April 1 to the end of October. Last admissions 5.30pm; price £2.20. Point Hill, which Henry James rented before moving to Lamb House, and the converted oast house at Doucegrove where Sheila Kaye-Smith lived, are privately owned and not open to the public.

Suggested Route: Lamb House is on the corner of West Street and Church Square. Park and head uphill towards St Mary's Church, which has a stained glass window of the Nativity given by E F Benson. He persuaded the artist to include in it a portrait of his beloved Welsh collie dog, Taffy. Lamb House is a little to the west of the church, round the corner from the Mermaid Inn. Addicts of the Mapp and Lucia novels, wishing to identify the homes of the inhabitants of 'Tilling' and the shops they visited can obtain a map of the town Benson based on Rye from the Martello Bookshop, 26 High

Lamb House, Rye.

Street. With map in hand a tour of Tilling can be undertaken. When it has been completed take the A268 road, leaving Rye at the Land Gate. As the road runs up Rye Hill, look out for a narrow turning on the right with a small sign reading `To Point Hill'. The road is private and it is best to park on Rye Hill and walk. Among the various houses is Point Hill from which, in 1897, Henry James had splendid views of the roofs of Rye and the sea beyond.

Continue on the A268 through Peasmarsh and a couple of miles further on turn left on to the B2088 through Beckley then on the B2165 to Horns Cross. Fork left on to the A28 and a few hundred yards along, just after Tanyard Farm, turn left again. The little Roman Catholic chapel Sheila Kaye-Smith and her husband built in their garden is on the corner of the lane and her grave is in the churchyard. A little way along the lane, which is private, a public footpath skirts Little Doucegrove, the converted oast house in which they lived. Return to the A28, head south to Broad Oak and return to Rye on the B2089 through Udimore.

HENRY JAMES 1843-1916

THIS major figure in the history of the novel was an American who fell in love with Europe. His parents had taken him abroad as a child, and after Harvard, where he decided he would become a writer and not a lawyer, he went on the first of many trips to Europe.

His great loves were France, Italy and Switzerland but it was in England that he settled in the late 1870s. He lived for some years in Bolton Street, just off Piccadilly in London, then in Kensington and Chelsea.

He fell in love with the little town of Rye and in 1898 bought Lamb House and filled it with his friends in the summer months. It was there that his later novels, *The Wings of the Dove* (1902) *The Ambassadors* (1903) and *The Golden Bowl* (1904) were written. In them he returns to his major theme – the contrast between ebullient but uncultivated Americans and cultured Europeans whose civilisation was in economic decline – which he used to such effect in *Roderick Hudson*, *The American* and the exquisite *Portrait of a Lady*.

James's novels are never out of print and a number, including his well known ghost story, *The Turn of the Screw*, have transferred successfully to the stage and television.

By the standards of today they are sometimes slow going for his approach to the writing of fiction was that of a careful historian. He allowed into his novels and short stories only that which could be represented as something undergone or perceived by the characters in them.

James, who became a British subject in 1915, to display his support for the British cause in the First World War, left two novels, The *Sense of the Past* and *The Ivory Tower*, incomplete when he died a year later. Also uncompleted was the third of his three volumes of autobiography, *The Middle Years*.

Henry James by John Singer Sargent.
Photo: National Portrait Gallery

More than fifty years later he became one of only a handful of Americans to be immortalised in Poets' Corner in Westminster Abbey. At Lamb House visitors can see the downstairs rooms, slightly remodelled by James – he put in French windows – and the remarkably spacious garden which he loved. The garden room in which he used to write was demolished by a bomb in 1940. There is a project to rebuild it, supported by many of the American visitors who come to revere the master, even though he turned his back on America.

'I have been to the South, the far end of Florida – but I prefer the far end of Sussex,' he said.

E F BENSON 1867-1940

FIRST Radio 4 with the readings by Aubrey Woods, then the television series of *Mapp and Lucia* revived present day readers interest in the works of their creator.

Edward Frederick Benson was born at Wellington College where his father, Edward White Benson - Archbishop of Canterbury from 1882 - was headmaster. His first novel *Dodo*, supposedly based on the future Lady Oxford, created a sensation in *fin de sieclé* London. He followed it up with a stream of light novels, ghost stories, biographies and memoirs.

But it is in the six Mapp and Lucia books that his comic inspiration really comes into its own. In them he captures, with a deliciously sharp wit, the mood and flavour of English country town society of the 1920s. In three of the books, *Lucia's Progress, Trouble for Lucia,* and *Miss Mapp*, the town is Tilling, or rather Rye, to which Lucia moves from Riseholme - the Cotswold beauty spot of Broadway that is the setting for *Queen Lucia* and *Lucia in London*. Mrs Emmeline Lucas moves from Riseholme to Tilling in *Mapp and Lucia.*

Fred Benson first came as a guest to Lamb House when it was owned by Henry James, a family friend. Some years later he leased it with his brother, Arthur Christopher Benson, who spent the vacations from Cambridge there.

Arthur had almost a double life. He wrote bland novels and books of spiritual uplift which brought him a devoted following of women; but in his private diaries and in Cambridge college politics he was 'vehement, sharp and contemptuous'. He is chiefly remembered now for having written the words of *Land of Hope and Glory* to fit the music of Elgar's Pomp and Circumstance March No 1.

Fred Benson loved Rye and after Arthur's death lived there most of the time. He became a magistrate and was Mayor of Rye from 1934 to 1937. In his closing years he completed an autobiography, *As We Were,* the second volume of which, *Final Edition,* was finished only days before his death in 1940.

SHEILA KAYE-SMITH 1887–1956

AND now for someone completely different. Little Doucegrove was the home in later life of a novelist who took herself seriously and set her stories in the splendidly varied countryside of Sussex.

Sheila Kaye-Smith was born in St Leonards and published her first novel, *The Tramping Methodist*, when she was twenty one. Her output was prolific. She averaged a book a year over a long period, but the quality is variable.

She made a considerable study of the psychology of the Sussex peasant and the Sussex dialect and had a thorough knowledge of farming.

In the churchyard of StTherese of Lisieux, the chapel they built in their garden at Little Doucegrove, Horns Cross, Sheila Kaye-Smith and her husband are buried.

A frequent theme in her work was man's hard struggle to wrest a living from the land. She portrayed it as a bitter struggle, unrelieved by any vestige of humour.

One of the novels that brought her fame and some fortune was *The End of the House of Alard* published in 1923. The Alards were a real family of some antiquity, with tombs in Winchelsea church. It is set in a real countryside, and Conster Manor, the home of the Alards, and the farms around are lovingly described.

Two of Sheila Kaye-Smith's novels, *Joanna Godden* and *Susan Spray* were reissued by Virago Press in the 1980s, and the film of the former, made in the 1940s, has been on television in the 1990s. Although very much a regional writer with not a single book set outside Sussex, she has an enthusiastic following on the other side of the Atlantic. All her original manuscripts, letters, notes and papers are in the United States, most of them in the archives of the University of Texas.

She was a devout Anglo Catholic and married Theodore Penrose Fry, a curate at the church she attended at Hastings. In 1929 they were both received into the Roman Catholic church and in the garden of their home at Little Doucegrove they financed the building of the little church of St Therese of Lisieux. In its churchyard they are both buried.

Sheila campaigned energetically for the protection of the countryside she loved and for the establishment of national parks.

MORE WRITERS IN SUSSEX

WILLIAM Blake poet, artist, prophet and visionary, lived between 1800 and 1803 in a cottage opposit the Fox Inn at Felpham, near Bognor Regis. Here he wrote *Jerusalem* and also ejected a couple of drunken sailors from his garden with the words: 'Damn the King, damn all his subjects, damn his soldiers for they are all slaves'.

For this outburst Blake was charged with treason and tried at the Assizes at Chichester. He was acquitted and soon afterwards left Felpham for good.

THOMAS Paine, writer and revolutionary, lived at Bull House in the High Street of Lewes when he was serving as a somewhat unsuccesful excise officer. He married his landlord's daughter and emigrated to America in 1774. Persecuted and little thought of in England, he contributed by his ideas to the independence movement in America and the revolutionary stirrings in France. He published *The Rights of Man* in 1790, and was tried for treason *in absentia* and outlawed from England for some of the seditious passages the book contained.

ALFRED, Lord Tennyson, appointed Poet Laureate in 1850, built Aldworth House on Black Down, a remote spot on the Surrey/Sussex border near Northchapel. He moved there to escape the many sightseers who invaded his privacy when he lived at Farringford on the Isle of Wight. Aldworth House is privately owned and not open to the public. It can be approached from the public footpaths that skirt Black Down.

JOHN Galsworthy, novelist and playwright, famous for his sequence of novels *The Forsyte Saga*, bought Bury House at Bury, West Sussex, in 1926. There he played the squire, generously by all accounts, and entertained his friends from the theatrical and literary world. The village is on the west bank of the Arun to the right of the A29 between Arundel and Pulborough.

SIR Arthur Conan Doyle, creator of Sherlock Holmes, moved to Little Windlesham on Hurtis Hill, Crowborough, with his second wife, Jean Leckie in 1907. Then the five gabled house with its red roof and chimney stacks was set in a stretch of open country running from the South Downs to Crowborough Beacon.

One of the first things he did, after changing the name to Windlesham House, was to add an enormous billiards room with huge window at each end. There he would entertain many of the great men of the day. Rudyard Kipling would come over from Batemans to yarn about India, Sir Edward Marshall Hall liked to discuss methods of detection and Arctic explorer, Stefannson, would plan future expeditions, laying out his maps on the green baize of the table. The house, now called Windlesham Manor, has been a registered residential care home for a number of years.

WILLIAM HENRY HUDSON, naturalist and novelist was born in Argentina of American parentage but became a naturalised British subject in 1900. In *Nature in Downland* he gave a detailed description of the plants, flowers and wildlife of the South Downs. He stayed when he could in Worthing and is buried in Broadwater cemetery.

THOMAS HUXLEY, biologist and teacher, was in failing health in the 1880s and needed to leave London. He had a house built for him in Staveley Road, Eastbourne where he could rest after a lifetime devoted to science and anti-religious controversy. Huxley was a great defender of the Darwinian theory of evolution and engaged in a celebated argument on the question with Liberal Prime Minister William Ewart Gladstone.

S P B MAIS, writer and broadcaster on the joys of exploring England, spent the second half of his life in Southwick, near Brighton. His book on Sussex was first published in 1929 and reprinted up to 1950.

He was a guide for the new breed of weekend rambler coming out

The Hall, 48 Southwick Green, home of Sussex writer S P B Mais.

from London on the new fast electric trains. For them he wrote books of rambles in Surrey, Sussex and Kent. He lived first at The Hall, No 49 on Southwick Green, and then moved to Toad Hall, at the junction of Buckingham Road and Upper Shoreham Road.

ROBERT Tressell is famous for just one book, revered among socialists concerned about their history. *The Ragged Trousered Philanthropist* is based on the hard and precarious lives of working men in Hastings, where Tressell lived in the first years of this century. He died on his way to Canada in 1910. One of his addresses in Hastings, 115 Millward Road, has a plaque on the wall marking his stay.